AF488412

You Ruin Everything!

(and other lies I told myself in the first year of divorce)

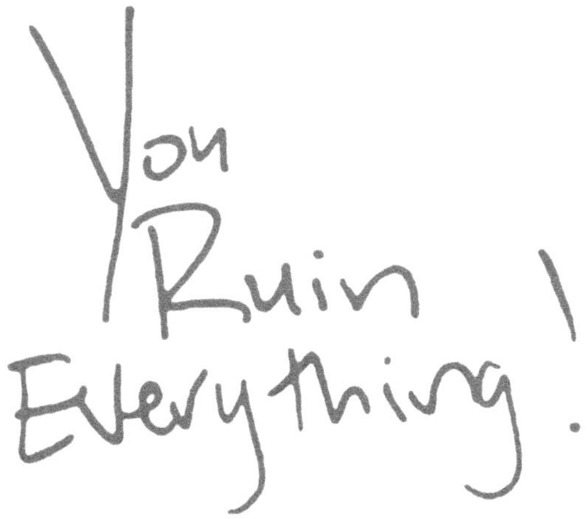

You Ruin Everything !

(and other lies i told myself in the first year of divorce.)

Kristin a. battersby

Published in the United States of America

Author photo: Colin Battersby Design: Randall Martin

Illustrations: Kristin Battersby

ISBN: 979-8-218-30450-8

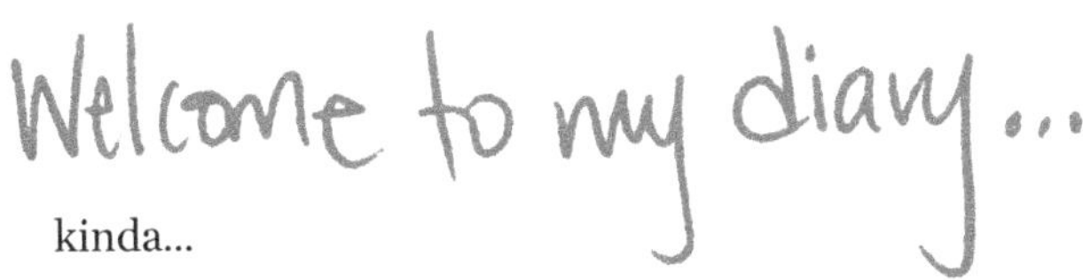

kinda...

I wrote these poems to pull myself out of the fetal position I often found myself in during my first year of divorce...For me, it got better after the first year...BUT-I could never ever have done this without the help of my amazing friends and family, animals (and afore mentioned fetal position).

Ruining everything to rebuild...turned out to be the right thing to do. For Me. For you it may look very different. There is no right way to change your life...but maybe this helps prepare you...

Here are some things I have learned...

Grief is not linear. I would feel great one moment and want to die the next

You divorce the same person you were married to...Conversations that used to be "easy" in the hallway become a battle over text and a screaming match on the phone

In the beginning, your ex is not your friend...you can be friendly...but not friends. Divorce is truly a business transaction...

One day one of you will meet someone...and the grief will hop right back into your heart like a flea on a dog. (Almost as pesky and itchy too)

Your in-laws may actually have never liked you...This was a huge shock to my ego...I've worked through it, but this was an unexpected twist.

Friendships you thought were yours...were actually his.

Give your former spouse whatever they ask for...financially...the money will come...tenfold. This was advice that was given to me during negotiations and it was so helpful.

Lastly-there is hope...I am lucky enough (TODAY) to get along with my ex husband. We laugh, cry and make jokes. We are happy for each other, and we are great co-parents. It took almost 3 years, but we are there, and I'm so grateful.

Hopefully he won't read this book...but I'm so glad you are.

Thank you...

—kb

Thank you....

to the many people who have carried me
through this process and who without their
support I could never have finished this book...

Carmen Cuba

Jeffery Battersby

Melissa Grisi

Emily Silver

Nicole Vani

Nicole Celaya

Erin Brown

Aleque Reid

Amy Johnson

Steph Farrar

Whit Brown

Lisa Belcher

Gina Mariani

Elna Baker

Brooke Burton

Sharon Leal

Adele + Levi Stanley

God

10

Contents....

for anyone
afraid to ruin
everything.

be still my heart
there's nothing left
an empty shelf
inside my chest

(woke up 1.14.21 to this ♡)

the
beginning
part...

Once Again
I'm feeling good
Trying to do
What I should

We have some fun
I'd thought "we're done"
And sure as fuck
You yuck my yum

There was no fight
You say goodnight
12 feet away
What did I say?

The mood is
gone
I thought
"we're done"
And sure as
fuck
You yuck my yum

We watch a show
I laugh you snore
I cry you sigh...
"when's this over?"

I find some space
Some peace some
grace
I feel some change
But I'm deranged

No war is won
No words unsung
I thought "we're done"

You
Yuck
My
Yum

I do the same
Again FOR change
Webster to claim
I've gone insane

I beat a drum
Threaten to run
You want to try
I know you lie

And weeks go by
The time doth fly
I think we're done
You yuck my yum

Am I to be
All of the things?
Strong and powerful
While I clean and sing?

So you can play
All night and day
Hiding in a cave
No marriage saved

But now I'm tired
I hear MY voice
I'm bored I'm wired
I have ONE choice

To live or die
This double sword
I vowed forever
I gave my word

But somewhere there
Should be a light
That grants a way
When things aren't right

That says " I DO"
Can be-"I'm Done"
No marriage saved

You yucked my yum.

 ♡ loss

Red leaves began my say goodbye
Hatha opening
A full moon sky

Native sound bath drawing near
Desert surrounds me
Thoughts are clear

Next was sleep pure-restless
Tossing, Turning
Ending us

Then smile and wave
through desert stores
Adele beside me
What's my course?

First tell a friend or two or
five
Envision freedom
Feel alive

Pass thirsty mountains heading west
Build strategy
Kindly at best

Would take nine days from then to say
I can no longer
Love and stay

With both hearts breaking, barreling
through
Bull in chinashop
(The shop is you)

Apologies
on our shared land
A beg a plead
To keep my hand

The day I got clear...

A calm washing right over me
Says i love you
But i found me

Sweet yoga how you open
  wide
  And make me say
  What's real inside

  By winter's moon i've
settled in
My new home-me
My heart within
Am-i-ca-ble my new found
word

No speaking now
  Your voice unheard
        And somehow
knowing all the while
That you and i will
End with smiles

That we are held no longer
one
And we are stronger
Happy. Done.

With divine evidence safely
moved
Right where i am
And it is good.

The house was empty
when i left
Lucy and lily knew
Jenny slept...
Typical

I forgot to tell you
I kissed your dad
goodbye
His ashes in a jar
labeled-Dad
I told him i was sorry

I took a picture of lily
Standing by the wall
covered in wood
Not just any wood...
wood you found around
Los Angeles....

Wood from our
first home-
wood with a pulse
Ours.

I forgot to tell you
I paid the gardeners
through OctoberI had no
idea talks like
this would be
So difficult later- no
longer stopping to talk
in OUR
Hallway

I forgot to tell you
I miss that...
I, Miss battersby
misses, Mrs stanley
It's still on my mail
Official

I forgot to tell you
I took the
"Don't worry bout a thing
Cuz every little thing gonna
be alright -love, bob"
Mug

I forgot to tell you that
I have not heard from your
mom or sister
These women in my life for
22 years and 5 months
Gone in just a moment...
it's ok, just...
Grief

I forgot to tell you
I remembered last
Thanksgiving...
How we swore we'd never go
to your sisters again
It felt like a connection we
had
knowing that was loving and...
True

I remember feeling protected
by you that day.

I forgot to tell you
Our kids are fucking amazing.
We did some real good...
Some damage too, but,
mostly
Good

I forgot to tell you
I will always love you
I will always miss you
I will always be here just...
Different

I forgot to tell you
I found a card i
gave you that read:
"One day you will
find this card in the
bottom of a drawer
And we will still be
in love" and...
I cried.

Do all things in love
Leal reminded me of that
But i forgot to tell you
I love you andrew,
just...

 ♡ loss

You ruin everything
That's what she said
She only talks
From one side of my head

You ruin everything
Tumbles and dreams
Dancing and shining
With no care it seems

You ruin everything
Remember when
I was a star and you
were my friend

You ruin
everything
I had a plan
You hid behind
Chasing man after man

You ruin everything
Why now so new
i 'll wait and watch
While you prove what you do

You ruin everything
Fraud liar cheat
Who would believe you
Just accept defeat

You ruin everything
Why do you cry
does what i'm saying
Make you want to die?

You ruin everything
What's that you say?
You

You ruin
everything
(a conversation
with little kb)

will take care of me
Now we can play?

You fight for everything
Kids me and you
I see a light in you
Something brand new

You ruin everything
Wasn't a threat
It was a warning Something
left unsaid

Hiding and fighting and

Pushing down time
I ruined everything
Now i will find

A u t h e n t i c factual
Bright shiny me
Ruining everything
Can't wait to see

To ruin takes courage
  It means you are strong
  You fight for what's
    better
  And move things
    along

          Peaceful and
            quiet and
            calm
        Let's undo
      I Accept this new
power
I invite you too.

I ruin everything
Someone once said
Upheaval and ruin
Much better than dead1
We will move through all
this
Finally set free
I will be you
And you will be me

I feel the shift happen
Death is my birth
I am so glad
That i listened to her.

I took your name
Out of my phone
Today

2 months ago
I made someone else
My emergency contact

One month ago
Andy became Andrew
Your profile pic from us to our kids

And today-Andrew
Became A S
as...I say goodbye to it all

The endearments
The nicknames
The inside jokes

I took your name
Out of my phone today
Your rugged hands off my heart

I placed the crystal
You gave me for my birthday
In our daughters room

I gave your bed
To a Russian mover
Your rug I left in the driveway

The driveway that
I pay for
And happily so that I can be free

I took your name
Out of my phone today
I took your name and now claim mine

Kristin Adele Battersby
Not stanley
I took your name out of my phone...

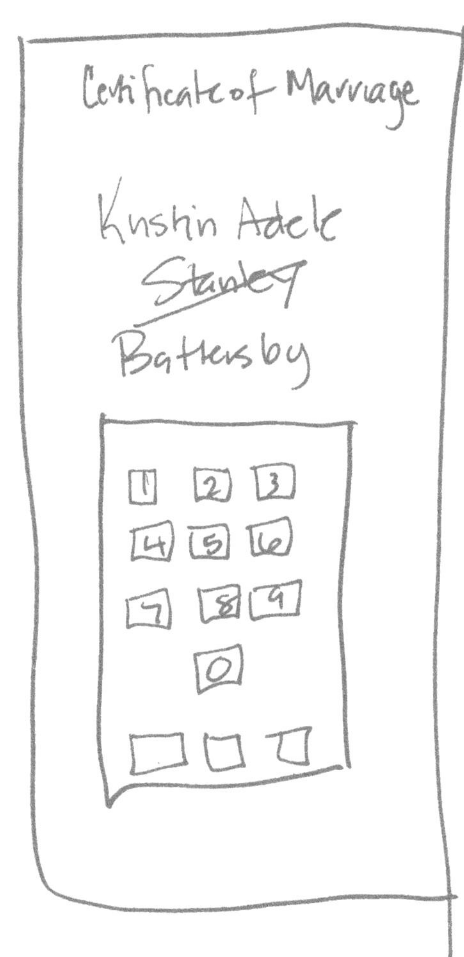

fix

I have an overwhelming urge
to fix things.
Not with a hammer and nails.
With my brain.

Silence between us is the
broken thing
That i want to spackle, paint,
and smooth over
No words from you, negative
or positive
Well that means i need to
get in there and mess with
something.

It's like plastic surgery
really...
It is made how it's meant to
be...but i want to change it.

i suppose that comes from a
life long dream of needing
EVERYBODY TO LIKE ME
please...........
Which is impossible...but
even as I type that, I feel like
it is possible.
Like come on, I am
ridiculously likable.

i want my freedom...yes,
But i also want you to need
me
Isn't that just the way?

In our marriage i was lonelier
than i am now in this 1600
sf flat
Gorgeous flat i might add
"You have really leveled up"
people have said
People who like me...
When i wake up in the
morning, i am ok

i am better than ok really i am
smiling and grateful
The birds, my new
roommates, sing to me, i feel
like it's spring my senior year
in hs
Almost done with this 18 year
stretch...this rollercoaster

Literally 18 years...planning
and plotting and convincing
you to marry me
Begging you to bend to the
norms that you really rather
would not have
But you did...i got pregnant
And you bent...

And you would tell her 16
years later that When she
came into the world
...life had meaning.
For the first time.

Where in the past 18 years of
our lives did shit fall apart?
So much pressure so many
miscarriages, bottles of
Wine
Tequila
Vodka
Sierra Nevada....god i miss
those celebration ales.
They come out right about
now...
The first case was always the
sign of months of drinking.
And i couldn't wait to get that
ball rolling.
Taking a trip, not taking a trip

Fights, brawls...buzzed
driving is drunk driving...that

always got me..
Numb
That's what killed us.
Our need to be numb.

Once the booze was gone,
isolation became our
medicine...
Not together in our
isolation... that became the
wedge
Rejection---constant fucking
rejection

"I am writing a script with
Sharon"
"You are so hollywood"

"Can you believe Trump is
blah blah blah"
"Well he has a point"

"I was reading this article"
"Ha, you read the whole
thing? Wow"

What?

Why so contrary all the time.
Condescending
Lighting the gas...

i've been holding my breath-
i've been counting to 10 over
something you said.

i'm fucking quoting a Cyrus.
And it feels so right.

So this feeling...this need to
fix...i release you.
You need a bed frame...i am
not going to buy it.
i've been holding you up for
18 years.

the I'll never
be enough
part...

I miss the days
When I would cross my legs
And they'd fall like
Greta Garbo

No chunk a bunk
To cause my brain funk
And doubt myself
Be my own foe

I miss the scale
That would tell a tale
That made me feel
Like i was just fine

The number so low
Would soften the blows
And all of the world
Could be mine

I miss size 2
And 4 and you
The cult that made
Me shrink so small

The gatherings chats
Weighed food measured fats
And talks of god
Life, romance and all

I miss the way
I would breezily chasse
From my closet to
The SF streets

Without a fear
Of how i appeared
Just tiny, brave
sexy young me

I miss trying on clothes
Everything fits so loose
And my style was
Clever and fun

No size large or size ten
Causing my head to spin
About who i am
"What have i done"

I miss confidence
My long lost friend
And how she held
My young unspotted hand

She still talks to me now
"Love yourself here is how"
Now i look in the mirror
Say "I understand"

I miss you most of all
My strength, heart, and fall
Somehow all of this
Intertwined

How we change day by day
And no longer have sames
It's all fizzled and
Left far behind

I miss the time
Under olive tree chimed
I was yours you were mine
Til the end

But even that day
I felt fat, so afraid
I remember that most
Truth can bend.

I miss what lies ahead
Already i dread
Weddings, birthdays
Casual so and so's

Where you'll have on your arm
Someone younger with charm
Whose legs cross
Like Greta Garbo

 ♡healing

Zero to sixty in 5 seconds
It appears to me that we should stop
Pedal to the metal ya burn rubber on me
I'll be on top

Wrote that song in 1999.
The year we were all gonna party like it's...
Never partied.
Instead on the morning of 2000 Jan 1
My boyfriend and I broke up.
He moved to LA
I stayed in SF

And that was that. 2 years of
back and forth
should we shouldn't we
became...
Meh-we're just not.
And then I wrote more
songs.
All about him...

Kinda

I wrote them
with his ex
roommate.
His best friend.

Songs so passionate and
sexy and full of meta-
phors...

We recorded them in his
living room.
The tension was thick

I weighed 116 lbs soaking wet then
And my worth was skyrocketing.
That's me in the corner...

With a scale
Measuring my self worth by a number that
appears
Each time i step on it...
        roulette with my emotions.

When did my self evaluation become based
on some
        Conditional self love?
            When did i become obsessed with
                How very badly i needed you to
                like
            Me

And how if you don't like me
It's obviously because i am carrying a little
extra weight
Proportionally...you would tell me...

So that's "good."

One hundred + sixteen

But
    Now
      even when you say "good"
    I hear
    "Could be
better."

Grief is...klip klopping
Back of mind
Feeling beauty
Mostly dread

Floating lightly
Til it comes
Take me over
Wish for death.

Grief is...

private
Lonely, sure

Can be conjured
In quiet storm

Or in Stillness
Of a song

That a friend
Sends
Because
They thought Of me

And then i realize
I am sad

And, worse...
it is obvious

And people
love me

And think of me
In music

And i am washed over
By sorrow...

Just briefly
Enough

to be reminded
That it is good

To feel

Something...

the i miss
him part...

It's too soon to write about
you
I can barely stand near
I come so unglued
Knees buckle with fear

You laugh at my jokes
You get every one
Your pants fit so nicely
I wonder who won?

It's too soon to miss you
I just left last week
I felt so much power
Today I feel weak

It's too soon to be friends
I so like your face
The past 3 months flew by
No tender embrace

It's too soon to visit
The house was once ours
To go through old stories
And lose all the hours

It's too soon to
wander
My head to your
lap
To tell you
my daily
Gripes of this and
that

It's too soon to write how
I've made big mistakes
And look for the rug and
sweep,
for our kids sake

It's too soon to recall
Our memories right now
I can barely see you
Without wondering
how?

It's too
soon to
listen
To
your

chit-
ter
chat
I'm
just busy
thinking
"I bought you
that hat"

It's too soon to
casually

Text you hello
We used to tell secrets
And share a pillow

It's too soon to say
It was all worth the pain
Or remember how we
laughed
Without refrain

It's too soon dear Andy
To write you this poem
I'm living on orange
drive
And you're in our home

It's too soon to wrestle
This tug at my heart
Is this the real ending
Or a brand new start?

It's too soon to think about
Somebody else
But I'll get there soon I
know
First-love- my-self

It's too soon to wrap this up
So much to say
But I'm glad we stopped
and said Hi
Just Today.

Answer my calls...

I appreciate me,
I appreciate you
I'm not mad
Sometimes i really miss you,

and the man that I wish
you had turned out to be
I'm not mad
But, fuck, sometimes I am lonely

All the hammers and nails
and things that you found
our home felt so full
with no penny
around

all the jokes that
we had
between just us two
how hard it is to laugh
Without sharing with you

all the times that you
didn't answer my calls
Could I have just shrugged
it off
let it go let it fall

all the times that
I asked you to go
for a walk
Or to fuck or to eat
then felt drained
when you talked

What is my fault
what did I do?
I know...I neglected
So much of you too...

I know I became
complacent-set free?
When I became
"most selfishly" me

but I read somewhere
in a book called untamed
That knowing inside
Just won't let me stay

It's the gift that I'm giving
    the kids and to you
    It's the setting us free
    to see what we can do

  I don't want to raise children
To feel they must stay
just because they signed paper
because "it's that way"

I don't want to raise children
who silence their pain
then muzzle themselves
and look with distain
    How two people who once

    Loved each other got mad
      at so Many nothings

    I know it's so sad.

    I know that we feel it
      we have to, we do
  But I cannot wait to be done,
    simply, over you !

I don't think it will happen
not really, not soon
but I know that i'll change
and my dear so will you...

One last request
As I bid you adieu
Please stop looking
As good as you do

This aging so gracefully
And better with time
Is fucking with my head
And making me pine

For something that wasn't
For a past in my dreams
For a snuggle a cuddle
A fuck and a scream

For a partner a lover
A joker a friend
For something I let go of
In this bitter end

Please stop smiling
The way that you do
The twinkle in those eyes
Blinding many and few

And please stop pretending
You wish I was there
You hated our marriage
It's beyond repair

I'm not bitter sweetie
I'm happy for you
It's all just unfair
When you look like you do.

I don't like the word
divorce
I just wanted a front porch
To rockabye sweet baby
All the day

I don't like the way it
feels
Waking up, forget it's
real
Hurry up, wait, sign
papers
Right away

I don't like the big
headaches
Greet me every time
i wake
Is it grief,
dehydration,
Or just me?

I don't like paying the bills
Water, power, taxes, cell
I just want to grow old
Wild and free

Not what we foresaw at all
Grandchildren 'round us,
tall
Playing singing laughing
Telling tales

Not at all what i once knew
In my heart that grew and
grew
That i'd love you and you
felt same no fails

But i do like my new place
My grey hair, my sweet face
Strong thighs, soft lips,
round rump
Mine all mine

And i do like all the sounds
That surround me, peace
i've found
Hallelujah finally
I can shine

It was not so long ago
San Francisco picnic, show
Singer, actor, writer
Young were we

THAT for sure was our
sweet place
Twinkled eyes and smooth-
in face
    We began something
    We couldn't see

Two of the most shining
lights
Young and funny, smart and
bright
We have raised and they are
So divine

How could we have ever
known
Who they'd be when they
were grown
We must have done some-
thing right
Sometime

So I still hope that rocking
chair
Waits for us to laugh and
share
Bound by law no more
But deepest friends

Grandchildren around us
tall
Listen to our stories- all
Grateful that we found a
Peaceful end.

missing you

god damn it!
I woke up
missing you
today

best friends cat is
in the freezer
coyotes took max
away

i can breathe
and i can move
but i can't hug
myself

YOUR hugs (when genuine)
were warm/kind
not off the
shelf

vinyasa flow
with destyne
while emily's
away

nothing's in
it's
prop-
er

place
when i wake up
this way

carmen and i
talking homes
with hills surrounding
us

trees and brush and
fear and joy
fire questions, god we
trust

scrambled eggs
and english muffin
buttered perfect,
right

while the middle east
is suffering
I binge shows all
night

ridiculous, this life,
this darkness
looming while we
dance
randomly flashback
to times

while naked,
we made
plans

then back to mundane
sunday practice, aimed
to bring me
calm

and thinking that
I made mistakes
god damnit, wake
on,on

justine recorded
what i wrote
it melted, healed my
heart

her cadence, flowy
here... not there,
it blew my mind
apart

why would i ever
leave LA
so full of light and
art?

why would i follow you
up north
where we first joined our
hearts.

i want to be so far away
from you,
from this, from
us

god damnit! i woke up today
and needed you
to love

You wished me well today
I heard your voice in the text

And I know you meant it
You wished me well without saying
Go to hell
You said you had
been ok.

I lost my shit I
know
It's not easy
talking to me
Talking to you

And why'd you
steal my neighbor
gal pals
From me?

They're Fraulein
Maria.
I'm the dead mom
Replaced.

But she said no
never
You will never be
replaced
Mom.

I signed papers today.
And you
You wished me well.

I ordered food from yummy
And looked to see if

Your favorite
vegan wraps
were there

Sold out.

I remember I'd
feel so proud
when
I surprised
you with
Vegan food

All while rolling
my eyes

And now David
Bowie plays
In my beautiful
living room
And I had a good
week at work

And I don't miss you
But you you wished me well.

Is it my wounding
Is it my wounds
But no
I know I knew I am

Doing what I knew I needed to all along.
And you
You wished me well

Dear Diary,

Dear diary,

I just went on instagram
Kids posted something funny
And I am crushed because I have no idea what room they are in
What chair that is in the home i lived in
And what does pog mean
Ha

Inside jokes I am no longer a part of
At all

I want a drink
Or to die
Or to time travel
Or to not be in this body today

I love you kb

 ♡ loss

february 14

Twenty two years
Of Valentine's
This first alone
Was fucking fine

Showered with love
From friends afar
Went for a drive
And passed some bars

Where lovers drank
And laughed a lot
And in their ranch
Dipped Tater tots

It brought me back
To peaceful us
To heart burst love
Fallen to dust

It made me crave
Something much more
As I walked by
Eyes on the floor

But all around
The green on trees
The heart shaped boxes
Skinned up knees

I found myself
Alone again...
Naturally.
That's all the end

the confident
part...
our

I cried last night
It'd been a while
Watched nomadland
Thought of your dad's smile

I dreamt last night
That you thrived
Living in a loft
You looked alive!

I dreamt last night
Of a secret kiss
Then longed for feelings
I won't let me miss

I felt last night
Some old some new
I lied today-
"what if my ONLY love was you?"

I sit right now
And miss the past
Daydream of you
But it won't last

You'll text me soon
With something harsh
I'll write and dance
Protect my heart

I wept last night
Didn't think i could
I cried last night
And it was good...

I am silver
I am grey
And without you
Im ok

I am happy
I am sad
And without you
Not so bad

I am here
I do shine
And without you
I am fine

I am day
I am night
And without you
I'm alright

I am quiet
I am loud
And without you
I'm allowed

To be me
Without you
I keep saying it.
Do you too?

Without you
There is me
Even though
It's hard to see

Without you
I am free
free 's expensive
Actually!

I am stylie
I am me
And without you
I can see

who the
fuck am i ???

I AM
FREE!

I am funny
I am light
And without you
Dyn o mite!

I am lonely
I am warm
And without you
I can form

I am sunshine
I am rain
And without you
I have pain

I am sorry
I am mad
And without you
Often glad

I am every
I am all
And without you
10 feet tall

I am empty
I am full
And without you
My heart pulls

I am handy
I can fix
And without you
No more tricks

I am one
With my source
And without you
I'm a force

Explore

I'm exploring me today
Every twist and turn
Downward dog and upward
cobra
For my soul i yearn

When i'm feeling weary
Troubled tired or woe'd
My mat comes to meet me
Grounding through my toes

Even if it's midnight
Anxious stressed and sad
A simple savassana
Re routes my neuropaths

Thoughts that wandered
aimless
Riddling my brain
Turn to mush with just a
breath
Dribble down the drain

Meet ME on the mat
That's all i need to do
When my heart is achey
And the moon is blue

Writing heals my dizzies
Dancing heals my soul
Tricky to get to that spot,
but yoga makes me whole

Yoga brought me right here
Yoga takes me through
If it weren't for yoga
I'd still be with you

Twisting more to fit you
Turning at your call
Lying to myself all day
Too afraid to fall

One month straight of yoga
One month followed two
One more month i see me
And i'm no more with you

And yoga take me further
I trust you, need you so
When i am yearning for me
I know just where to go

I can't hide from me with
you
I'm authentically me
I never knew this person
I'm happier, I'm free.

I wanna be a
Big boobie yoga girl
Big booty dance
And twirl

Big lashes
Mama son
Big baller
Megatron

Big sassy
So and so
Big singer
Rap and flow

Big tasty
Yummy thing
Big money
Emerald ring

Big serving
Apple sauce
Big fucking
Lady boss

Big munchy
Crunchy gal
Big juicy
Bestest pal

Big hearted
Listening
Big eyeballs
Glistening

Big boobie
Yoga girl
Big booty
Dance and twirl

Ugh, my friends is, not a
word
A vibe... it's how I feel
When I am uncertain
And nothing seems real

This mind can be dangerous
The chatter so loud
The weakness for outbursts
My head in the clouds

My fever is normal
But how my blood boils
I reach for my cell phone
For trouble and toil

I light all the candles
The flicker the flame
I call my ex lovers
To forget your name

I wander down store aisles
Mask covers red lips
I wear pleather pants
I sway my sweet hips

I buy myself flowers
I treat myself kind
I call my ex lovers
To reframe my mind

I buy pretty colors
To fill my new house
I rearrange furniture
Heavy now with no
spouse

I empty my wallet
I bare my brave soul
Find fetal position
Seeking warmth from
the cold

I pray to a goddess
A spirit a light
I read brene-kinda
Then turn out the light

I write and I write and
I write til I'm sore
I call my ex lovers
To even the score

I look at new houses
I dream of what's next
I drink too much caffeine
I delete your texts

I sleep in a new bed
I wake to the rain
Outside my new balcony
My heart and mind sane

I zoom 12 step meetings
And yoga and friends
I'm comfortably living
This time with no end

I count all my blessings
I check on my mom
I buy a new journal
I write a new song

I perfect my playlist
While resting my feet
I look at old pictures
It all seemed so sweet

I relish my friendships
Each and every one
I pray for you Andy
When all days are done.

But I had the courage
I'm so god damn brave
Myself I have ruined,
 My love I have saved

My socks are balled up at the foot of my bed
Tucked in so tight...
So like, I can't really smooth out the blan-
kets
Unless I unmake the bed

Oh...did i tell you?
I make the bed every morning now.
Now that winter is here
and , well, there is no one sleeping late
In my bed

MY bed...
A queen
Brand new
The smartest financially irresponsible
purchase
I've ever made...

I make my bed every morning.

My mattress was not free-
But i feel free
When i put my meditation sounds on
And close my eyes at night
Socks on

I've been sleeping in my own bed for a
while.
Since last winter
We thought it was fine.
We thought we were
"that couple"

We didn't
like to
snuggle in
bed anyway.

My Christmas lights are up
They're white this year
Can you imagine?
Remember the colorful lights you would
put up
Just to make me smile?
Even though you don't really like Christ-
mas lights

Damn.

Last night, i missed you
Lisa warned me-I'd miss the inside jokes
I thought-meh that's easy
I was wrong.

I made my bed

It's crispy out
Cold
Your voice on the other end of the phone
From my new home to our old home
It's colder

And

I know we will warm up
By Easter it will be gone
We will rise up

Make our bed(s)

My socks are balled up at the foot of my bed
Tucked in so tight
And, I'm ok with the lumps...

Even though I shouldn't
I still love the idea
Of nothing being about a single year

A new year?

All the same
Because there is no there there
But i am there,
and it is good...

Even though
I do be feeling lonely at times
And
I am aging and maybe

Not a new person yet

Even though
Money could run out
I could die of covid
And you could get $2 mil

I am still happy

Even though
I shouldn't be, i am
Serene

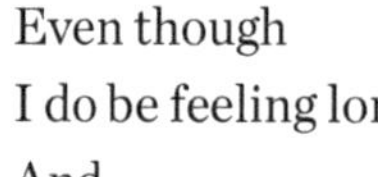

Even though
Words sound brand new to me
All the time

and i don't know you anymore

Is it just me?

does everyone who sepa-
rates
imagine they'll be killed
by choking, falling, heart
attack
by sword ex lovers wield?

does everyone just touch
themselves
in living room and hall
and fantasize about the fate
and wonder of it all?

does everyone make too
much food
the brain stuck on "for two"
and think about the funny
things
ex lover used to do?

does everyone wake up at 3
with darkness in side out
and get their water, just go
pee
then weep and stir
about?

does every-
one feel
confident
while
signing legal
docs
and imagine a time
when they
will see some brand new
cock?

does every gal make plans
to see
their boyfriends from the
past
Simply, ;) just to wish them
well, and hope
they think about that ass?

does everyone smile giddily
at all that they have done
to taste this bit of freedom
to see what they become?

does everyone feel lucky
dodging bullets left and
right
and fall asleep to old tv
shows
humming in the night?

does everyone in quiet
times
play chet baker so loud

or coldplay, dolly, frank
ocean
Gambino, beatles, round
and round

does everyone sponta-
neously
break out into a dance
on kitchen, dining, bath-
room floor
their feet princety prance.

does everyone look forward
to
the year, and pray, it pass
that ex lover will be ok
and also miss that ass?

does everyone make giant
plans
to write and film and play
to be a different person now
and every single day?

does everyone enjoy
the peace
of no regret-NOT
ONE
of being with their
raddest self
at dawn and set-
ting sun?

in this first year I feel the
love,
Rage, hatred, sadness too...
but i don't miss one god-
damn thing
about being with you.

There's a bump
On my nose
Am I special?

There'r freckles
In my eyes
Do I shine?

There's a Red
On my lips
Do you see it?

There's a light
In my heart
I am fine.

There's a sway
To my walk
Does it irk you?

There's a sass
To my tongue
Does it scare?

There's a longing
Inside me
To hurt you.

There's a lump
In my throat
When you're there.

There's a way
That you talk
Reminiscing?

There's a look
In your eye
Fa mil iar

There's a smile
And a stutter
I'm missing

There's a memory
Of you
Makes me purrrr

There's a bone
That I've got
To pick with you

There's a way
Subtle things
That you say

There's some tension
Panties start
To wrinkle

There's a time
That we longed
Night and day

There's a question
I'd like to
Pose to you

There's a whisper
A conjure
Some more

There's a place
I'd like to see
My garments

There's a place
On your
Hardwood floors

There's a truth
That is
Extremely boring

There's a family:
A wife
And some kids

There's a moral
Reaction
I'm storing

But my fantasies
Know
What we did...

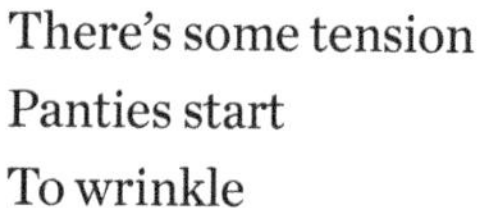

In da club

I'm in a different club now
The one with naked hands
The one with lonely
heartbreak
Who tries to understand

A club with lots of members
Each one a pensive look
A club with grieving mood
swings
In room with self-help
books

I am not
this clubs
leader
I didn't want
to join
I didn't think
I'd get in
I kinda flipped a
coin

My job now
is to notice
A finger on
left hand
A family
walking-
happy
A couple
laughing, grand

I see the glow
surrounding
New lovers on the street
A cup of coffee Sunday
A shyness first they meet

I look on-thinking fondly
Of when I first met you
And how I never ever
thought
This club was for us two

And surreal as it is now
I'm answering role call
Battersby, Kristin?
"Here" I say
My hand higher than all

I look around chairs empty
This club's not very fun
Each time a newbie enters
They say "what have I
done?"

I'm in a brand new club now
One day I hope to leave
And find a snuggly funny
guy
With heart right on his
sleeve

I thought it
would be longer
My finding a new
him
But something's
inching closer
My heart an open
hymn

Someday I'll
leave my club
mates
I'll never once
look back
And move on to a
new tribe
New rules: love,
trust, no lack.

the angry part...

If you decide
To get divorced
My friend
I'm warning you

FIRST, Plan and strategize
Your life
Grow strong SOUL muscles
Too

Only speak of how you
Feel
With folks you know you
Trust

Feel a twinge of
disbelief...
I beg you trust your
Gut

Think you've got it figured
Out
Like yours will look so
Different

Listen to your friends
They know
The ugly comes out in
Dividends

Conversely it should also
Be
Important, think it
through

Remember you are
divorcing
The one you were
Married to

The lackadaisical never
Minds
And casual charms here
There

Will show up now as daily
Harms
As critical/mean
Bewares

And even though
Each striking blow
Will sting and
Catch your breath

You will be eternally
Grateful
For canceling
"Til Death"

You'll find your tribe
They'll have your back
And front
and middle too

And hopefully
When time has past
The real you
Will come through

So pause and pray
And write and dance
And get your ducks
In row

For divorce is a dangerous
Game
Where lover now is
Foe

  faith

Please contact Gina
She'll answer all your q's
Please stop hyper-texting me
As I bid you adieu

Please stop lying
Is that asking too much?
Please find truth and meaning
Of both you're out of touch

Please stop faking deeply
That you really care
Please stop flaunting daily
That you still live there

Please stop begging, Andrew
It does not become you
Please stop acting like
Your so surprised boo hoo

Please stop your hard martyring
It's old -it's so passé
Please stop alluding to
The fault being solely me

Please stop using words
To seduce me somehow
Your manipulation has
Worked before but not now

Please stop tricking me
No words• some words• a text
I get so far away from you
What will you think of next

Please don't take my kindness
And turn me into weak
Please don't call me KB
When ever we DO speak

Please just let me move on
Answer emails, do your job
Please just sign the papers
So that we can move on

Please don't talk about me
In poetry and rhyme
I will stop now a s
You've used up all my time

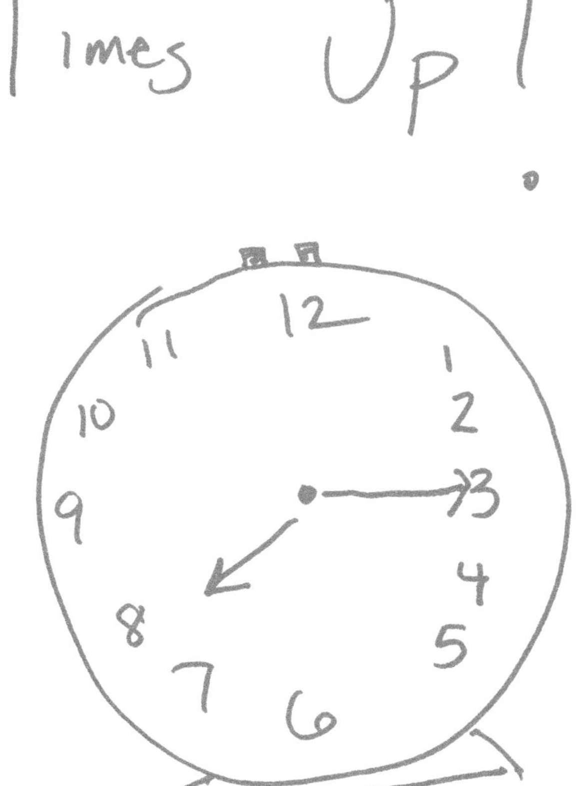

why

God the back and forth
today
Yesterday and days before
I can't fucking talk to you
I'm shutting the damn door

The murky muddy waters
here
Are just the very tip
Of what we need to uncover
Before the papers flip

And god i want to fix it all
For you, i guess for me?
I want to tidy up your mess
So i can become free

I want to tell you please
shut up
You're killing me so slow
And this is why i had to
leave
Just five short months ago

Holy shit and holy fuck
Can't believe that this is
me...
"Have your lawyer please
call mine
And please don't bother
me"

I know it's sudden i know
it's soon
You've told me many times
But what relationship were
YOU in
When I was deep in mine?

I call friends now because
my dreams
Remind me of our love
Of times we laughed and
fucked and teased
And shared our dreams
above

I ask them frankly tell me
why
I left again, again?
And they recite a list to me
Because they are my friends

Do you know not one of
them
Said wait, love are you sure?
When i said i am leaving
him
They said it's time my dear.

Thank god i write every-
thing down
To remind me of when
You lost your shit and i lost
mine
Over a simple question.

When i said playfully that
day
That we should go have sex
And you asked WHY so
willfully
I knew you'd be my ex

I laughed and tried my very
best
To deflate that reject
And called a friend or two
or five
"This is how god protects"

So now i'm begging
something big
To pull me from the flame
My heart it caves my throat
is closed
As i change my last name

Over, yes, the song is saying
I guess we're over too
And even with all evidence
I always will love you

Without you there would be
no him
No her no them no us
Hop in my car and drive
away
My sign FREEDOM OR
BUST

My nose is tingly as i write
As tears well in my eyes
I really fucking always
thought
That you would be my guy.

 ♡ release

day 69

since i said what i wanted.
Tomorrow is our 17 year anniversary.
I keep remembering everything good.
The laughter the vagueness
the monumental moments-
adele, levi...the day we found out about
each of them.
Our pain transferred to cells moved to
humans.

I never thought we would last.
Maybe i thought i didn't deserve love like
yours.
Maybe i ruined it all.
But i am more serene
and happy today
than i have ever
been.

That is something.

Day 69.
We were both born
in 69.
I always imagined
we were each others
bday gift.
Not growing old with
you...that is some
weird shit.
How did we get here.

Betrayal,
vagueness,
frustration,
confusion,

concussion,
alcoholism,
sobriety,
all the sex,
no sex,
deprivation,
punishment,
little tiny lies,
all the money,
no money,
buying selling foreclosing...lies.

Now when you are mad, i can't reach you.
You trusted me. I'm sorry.

Ive never been this serene ever.

There is nothing wrong with me.
I'm sorry

what not to do...

Yell at your kid
For something (they) said
Or worse
For something they didn't

Tell yourself lies
Create alibis
When you know
You
    were never present

Buy anything
they ask for because,
You are worried that they'll
    Grow to hate you

Fear being like dad
Because that happens when
You so very badly
    Don't want it to.

Stay up too late
Wishing this or that fate
on yourself or on him
        Or on them

Gossip and cry
And make up more lies
Even though you're quite
bad
        At telling them

A:pol:ogize
After time it seems wise
To just show
them
    Your words do have
meaning

Talk of your ex
In a tone less than kind
Knowing full well
You're
        being demeaning

Some better ideas
That WILL bring you good
feels
If not at least
you
    will Know you are trying

Just follow these thoughts
And No matter what you
will be
Content
        when you are done
crying

Seek what you like
In all people-They might-
Well, Some people will
Actually
        inspire you

Write letters and poems
And cozy your home
Breathe in and
breathe out
                Yoga: dance: too

Forgive and forget
Be honest don't fret
Don't pick
fights
        With your imagination

Give when you can
Of course, wash your hands
And make
life
    A new revelation...

the price of freedom...

This past two weeks
Have been fucked up
My head my heart
My toes I'm stuck

The middle was
The in between
The feeling nice
But acting mean

The ebb the flow
The way of life
The knowing
I am not your wife

The grief so real
No numb in sight
Inside my head
Ridicule and spite

Since you left town
And took our kids
My heart shattered
What's mine now his

And silence I can't
Feel or heed
I reach for food
For noise for greed

I get caught up
In someone new
Only to find
He's fucking just like you

No chase - no more
I've done that dance
I've weaved and bobbed
Stayed silent - trance

So fade away
I try not to
I have to think of
My kids too

I grasp and groan
Bargain and cry
Divorce a death
But I have died

While you seem fine
Whistling through
Your path is paid for
Sister, mommy too

So you won't need
To change a thing
Instead same same
I'll sell the ring

So I can pay
Your monthly fee
So I can finally
Be free

60

the are you
fucking kidding
me ? part...

What about bob...

Who is bob
Andrew?

Why is your first
half-jewish- red-head girlfriend's name
"Bob"...in your phone

Fine

It was not that
It's never been that
It's a feeling-andy
It's a knowing
That

No matter how i slice it
me/you/us
It's not connected
It's fractured
Lost
It's amazing who you keep
When the partnership is severed
It's an unspoken sentence
But like a really important one that should probs be
Spoken

Like a lot of the sentences
That just dangled
Ran on
Ended in a preposition and started with a but
Sigh

And just like that
I'm too fat
Fifty-two, have two cats
She's so cool and so fresh and so arty

I'm a boss
Own a house
Heart on sleeve, large size blouse
Big ole nose funny feet, fluffy body

And i try not to care
But i do-it's not fair
How i pay
So that you can fuck off...

But to perseverate
On you and YOUR fate
Is the perfect way
For me to get lost

So i'll cry, Eat some soup
Watch tv, Write some scoop
Dream of projects
With rivers run through it

And i'll not write a thing
About you suffering
No in fact i will finally
Pursue it

Wow i'm numb
now I'm sad
Now i'm sobbing, now glad

Remember our first park kiss
It was magic

But the truth is, old friend
I always knew it'd end
Just never knew you
Would be such a prick.

♡ loss   63

So i heard that you met someone new
I bet she looks a lot like you too
Made you a chair out of fucking bamboo

Merry Christmas...

Did you tell your mom, sister and friends?
Do they cheer that our chapter has ended
To our kids, what's the message you send?

Merry Christmas

the chair

So wait now do i pay for your dates?
And do you always make her wait
Do you return her texts super late?

Merry Christmas

Right now nothing makes me feel good
No loving words do what they should
But the sun will always shine through

Merry Christmas

For three years she was "bob" on your
phone
Now you finally can get her alone
Is it what you remembered, her moan?

Merry Christmas

I was happy the day i first heard
I was dancing and acting absurd
Til Adele told me that it was her

Merry Christmas

And the truth supposed to set
you free
But your truth is so fucked up
for me
What a fool i have been to
believe

Merry Christmas

So i'll send you cash twice every week
You're much smarter than most people
think
You've won this round you fucker you stink

Merry Christmas

Hookers and
prostitutes and parties
With men
Lying and cheating
and
Lying again

Searching not finding
but
Searching more still
Thankful I'm rid of you
Thanks to gods will

Tumbling and
stumbling and
Bumbling around
Omission, transmission
Car with no sound

Shaming and blaming
for
Just one small kiss
Fuck me, i fell for
decades
Of bullshit

Questions unanswered
And more questions
still
Who, what where,
when
And why, jagged small
pill

Fuck me, you fucked
WHO?
And NEVER touched
me

Shower by Shower and
anger
Now FREE...

From your curs-ed
energy
Lies cheats and thrills
How much of my money?
Panty Stuffed Bills

Bob on your phone while
You hit on my friends
Self doubt and torture
No end, no, no end

How did you think
I would never find out?
Why would my friends keep
your secret
Your out?

How could you do that
Then say to MY face:
"You ruin everything
KB find a place."

Rocky and dangerous and
cutting
Your lies
Abrupt and fractured and
shattered
Our ties

I see you smiling cheshire
cat
On face
You are a scoundrel
So easily replaced

A dime a dozen, Yep
That's what you are
How many women or men
And how far?

I'll let go resentment, the
sadness
leaves too.

I cant believe
That I WAS
married
          to
                  you.

curious   65

the am i ready
to date? part...

how's your heart?

What is this feeling
In my heart
Connection? Love?
Can't be apart.

Don't even know you
But feel so deep
Best friends? Lovers?
Consciousness seep...

You're quite the opposite
Of him I see
We look like family
But I want to be

More with you
A friend a pal
A snuggle buddy
Near you somehow

I thought these feelings
Would never come
It's been six months
Since the undone

But light and darkness
Overcome
I see you smiling
My heart feels warm

You text or chat...
I get the feels
Are you just friendly?
My head... or real?

I see us talking
Surfing too
Don't even know
What you like to do

I remember feeling
This light before
But editing me
So he'd want me more

But this I know
Is a new start
You text and asked me
How's your heart?

My heart is open
Tears are too
Can't wait to see
Much more of you.

Can't Quiet the Noise...

What is it about gardening day?
Leaf blowers bring up my heartache
And leaves and bugs and soil and dirt
So much crazy noise it hurts...

I play music to drown it out
But nothing kills its' surround sound
I take the route of bunny bugs
If you can't beat 'em join 'em? ugh...

I say hello, bring out the trash
I hope so hard the machine crash
Will come and save my soul from noise
Monday AND Thursday I've no choice

I'm not alone, my neighbors too
Feel trapped like animals in the zoo
My shoulders reach bottom of ears
My head is hazy eyes are tears

Anxiety brewing up inside
I want to yell please stop! please WHY!?
And illegal i thought they were
These machines that whine and whir

I seek now a quiet place
Inside my heart, i see your face
And then my heart starts whirling too
I'm like the blower, leaf is you

Intangible, too far to reach
But in my phone i hear you teach
I close my eyes i see you there
I feel you laugh, a gaze, aware

Then anxious comes back one more time
And gone is fantasy in real time
And i am stuck with whirring buzz
And i am seeking all your love

You are but one, i know a few
Right now i've got my sights on you
who can blame me? look at your face
My heart it aches slow is the pace

I plot and plan to see you close
My friends say wait let him move most
These games, i can't i just don't want
But you and me i dream it taunts

So hey how you and
hows your heart?
And why don't we
just walk to start
And see where one
foot takes us two
I hope it ends with
me and you

Holy shit, what can i say?
I've been shopping in aa
Looking for my new boyfriend
Will this searching ever end?

I can't help it all these men
Speak my language they and
them
Break me open word by word
Do they see me? I feel heard.

Then i start to break it down
I am old and ugly clown
Other women feel the same
He will never know my name

I grow angry bitter too
Resentment grows toward her
and you
My brother warned me and it's
true
"There'll always be someone
prettier than you"

But i am special i'm aglow
This is not my one man show
This is hope, recovery
I must shine internally

Truth be told i'm not ready
To be open wild and free
My heart healing slowly too
One day ready to love you.

First love me and grow and
grow
Then into the world i go
Letting go of what is MINE
Lean on god and i'll be fine

 ♡ faith

the thank god
i did this part...

How do i write a book
I think i'm on my way
Birds are chirping Spring has
sprung
and it's a perfect day

Woke with nothing brewing
My heads an empty vase
Lurking sadness stewing
Headache on my face

Neighbors talking loudly
La brea hums and squeals
Resting on my balcony
Spinning on my wheels

Sundays are my heartbreak
They're my healing as well
Kids arrive with lucy
Loneliness will quell

Work is easy for me
Gift of time and cash
Money flowing always
I rise from the ash

Do you think about me
With love instead of hate
I question this daily
But just couldn't wait

I've never been the breaker
The first to leave the dance
But the flame turned to a
flicker
My soul stood not a chance

And i could sit and ponder
A way to fix and stay
Fifty ways to leave your lover

This one works...I'm on my
way

Almost 2 weeks have passed
now
I haven't heard your voice
Except that time Adele called
I didn't have a choice

To hear you ask so sweetly
Mundane and simple task
I fear I'll never hear you
Without an angry mask

But still i fight for
freedom
My heart beats strong
and wild
I pray your mind will
open
I hope your pain is mild

I'll see you on the flip
side
At weddings or with
friends
Im grateful to you always
This lesson's at its end.

 ♡healing

These cordial hellos
And thoughtful goodbyes
These happy sweet convos
And tearful green eyes

These memories between us
They hurt and they burn
But I'd not trade any of them
For the love I have learned

Can we be friendly
Shit, can we be friends
Can this all blossom
From our marriage end?

I am here for all of it
Every last drop
From bitter to hatred to
Laughter non stop

And I'm sure we'll fumble
And tumble and cry
But to think- life without you
I would rather die

You've been by my side
Twenty two point five years
Through the drinking and eating
And spending my fears

You've been a great dad
To our amazing kids
And I'll never question
The hard work that we did
We put so much in it
But took way more out
And the end of this love
Brings a new one no doubt

I see a future
Where we celebrate
Weddings and birthdays
And other such fates

And I'll always love you
No way that I won't
But husband and wife
It just is our don't

I'm writing a book
About you and me
It's all written poems
It's setting me free

I hope that you like it
Take it what it is
And we will stay kind
Til the end of this shiz

Pandemic divorce
How cliche how mundane
It really just sped up
The suffering and pain

We put our love through
The test of all time
And this isn't a failure
More-a claim of what's mine

My heart and my soul
Will always be with you
Through Adele and Levi
Our souls will live through

And I am so grateful
And a little bit scared
Of what she will look like
And how I'll compare

But just for today

I will cherish our chats
I will take them for this
And not turn them to that

I'll show up and support
Your decision to be
Just who you are
And love me for me

This goodbye turned farewell
Is but just the tip
Of this travel through romance
As we end our trip

So thank you dear Andy
For showing up now
To replenish our ties
And show our kids how

We'll be better for it
That's what you said
And I couldn't agree more
Though our tears shed and shed

The good stuff is coming
Let's hang onto that
We're already better
Our hearts/minds intact

It's hard to end this one
I've so much to say
But I'll save it for you
On another day

I know there are no coincidences
I'm very very sure
Cuz when i look out my window
My memories are stirred.

I hear sounds i used to hear
When i was little me
The same birds, same whirring saw
The sway of the same tree

Rhododendron-Pepperipo
Just like on Versailles
Comfort me in my new home
As god picks up my wails

How can i ever think that there's
Nothing up above
Showering me with abundance while
Covering me with love

How can i claim back my will
When somewhere in between
Is a quiet conversation
Let go you're no machine

The music that i used to play
Wrapped up inside
my heart
friends text, face-
time and call and
post
It's all a brand new
start

When i feel lonely,
sad or mad
I look outside the
pane
And recognize i'm

where i'm meant to be
Here... once again

I fight i yell and time travel
I am so fucking mad
I resist so that quiet voice
Begins to hold my hand

But look around it whispers here
And grab hold of your heart
You're held kb you're loved so much
And it's a brand new start.

I don't mind
This empty nest
My beating heart
My pounding chest

I wake up happy
Better, best
Inside my cozy
Empty nest

I don't mind
You've flown away
And he's with him
And there he'll stay

We only have
But just one day
So fly and stay
And slay and stay

I don't mind
My lonely thoughts
Like do they like me
Do they not

I sleep fine
I slumber best
And I don't mind
My empty nest

I've made lots of room

What is that sound?
A bird in the trees?
Childhood is flashing
Loving memories

Lake time with family
And friends and between
Laughing and talking
Time fleeting
It seems...

This place is so special
My heart and my mind
Making new memories
Leave bad ones behind

He never liked it here
He really tried
I came without him
That's when we died

Now i long for him
Sober on the grass
Now i wish we could have
Changed our sad past

Or is it feelings
I miss about us
Pretending reeling
Missing the fuss

Twenty three years
Same lips meeting mine
One and a half years
He's still on my mind

Its not about money
Never really was
It was about loneliness
It was loss of love

It was about needing him
To be my best friend
It was about craving more...
It was time to end

Now looking around me
I see all grey hair
Like me i am grey, but
Not old and still fair

Still in this little town
The one he disliked
I feel closer to him
Especially at night

I see older couples
I wonder i say
I bet i'll be alone
Til my dying day

And that seems to sit
right
With me in my heart
But that's just today
Each day a new start

So i'm off to my friends
To snack and to play
And admire her part-
nership
It works well someway

So maybe there's hope
For me after all
For now i'll get ready
A walk, run a crawl...

Toward hope and my future
Toward lips touching mine
Toward sharing a cabin
To love so divine

I know it is out there
I'll find it so soon
My heart is wide open
I've made lots of room

the legal
stuff part...

Day is short...
Ending soon
I wait til moon hangs high

To dive into some Netflix
solo Chilling,
I won't lie

I make these rules
In my own home
To set a bar
so low

And numb myself
From what's to come
Closed eyelids start the
show.

The last five nights
I've dreamed of you-
And me, we're building
things

We've canceled out
Our shit divorce
I put on
all my rings

We're talking lots
And wondering how
To manage what we've done

We're laughing ghosts
The end is post
Our vows are now undone

I've talked to some
Who've been right here
The same place i now sit

They too had dreams
Of their ex loves
They too wandered in shit

It's healing, yes
To hear that I
Am truly
not alone

But lonely, sure,
I do feel that
Inside my low bar home

The sun is high
I wait for night
So i can binge and numb

But in my dreams
God damn it, mean....
You and i we are still, one

My dad he quotes
Walt Disney's words,
"A dream's a wish your
heart makes"

I'm not so sure,
It feels more like,
A dream is a wish your
heart breaks....

I saw you real life,
No feels caught
My heart beats calm with
truth

I forge ahead
Discomfort big,
Turn blind eye to my youth

1998 decisions made
 in places
We were young

We danced-drifted
Tried our best
But truth, like moon it
hung.

Our lawyers slap
Each others hands
This game goes on and on

And finally we'll sign one
day
When all is said and done

Amazing how this whole
thing works
From moon to setting sun...

One page to say
"I'll marry you"
Forty five to say "I'm Gone".

My name

In fifteen minutes
I'll go from Stanley
To Battersby

23 years of experience
Enveloping 8 years of
Confusion and misery

13 months of legalese
To erase 17 years
Of "marriage"

2 kids 2 dogs 2 cats
A bearded dragon
A rat

Endless unfinished projects
Couples therapy, retreats
Cheating in Vegas

2 years of separate bed-
rooms
5 years of no intimacy
Endless mornings of coffee

Coffee I would wait for
Longingly for the beep
And he would cut in front
of me

10 years of embarrassment
Drunkenness, shame
Name calling

11 years of worry
For Adele and what she saw
How she would be

7 years of worry
About levi his bitten nails
Down to nubs

1 year and 3 months almost
To the date
Of legal divorce

23 years of Roller coaster
rides
Vague text messages
No responses

6 years of longing to
Be married to him
Begging, knowing…

It was not right
Chasing shouldn't be part
Of courtship

One year of breaking up
2000 Jan 1
Y2K
Endless sleepless nights
So many hangovers
So many drunk drunk
drunks

And just like that
I'm KB. Thank you
Mardress SS admin…

This is me NOW
I'm crying at the
Social security office in
Pasadena

the i never
could've done
this without my
friends part.

New Room mates

My roommates are
new
All different each
one
From Ethan to
Barack to Brene
To Psalms

They don't really
pay rent
But do feed my soul
From Sieghart to Battersby
Cleo to Tolle

I personally know them
From paper to page
Elena to Shakespeare to
Michelle to Haye

They don't beg for attention
I seek them... I crave
From Demi to Glennon
The Lonely the Brave

I'll never be hollow
While these guys are here
They call without muffle
They draw me in...near

Still I open pages
And pick on myself
I'll never be like them
I'll dust on the shelf

I'll crumble and falter
Not NY Times Best...
I'll neglect my author
I'll raise up my fist

Or maybe just maybe
I'll open my heart
And fill all the pages
Let foes pick apart.

I'll shrug at their comments
I'll roll through the town
I'll not pay them homage
I'll adjust my crown

And sometimes just sometimes
I'll glance at my face
And hope I'm your roommate
In whatever place.

And you will crack open
And laugh/ugly cry
At all that I've told you
Gasp giggle and sigh

My roommates are new
All different each one
They're giving me courage
To finish undone.

In this life I am blessed with amazing friends
Ones who stand by my side til the very end

Sharon She comforts me when I'm low
She sees me accepts me, my every flaw

Lisa knows me best of anyone
She laughs and reminds me where i come from

Carmen so funny, so solid my sis
Dear us, how we found each other through all of this

My mom is my warrior my superstar
She's sassy so mincing words won't get you far

Aleque she's brilliant like twice her age
She lights up a room and she's so fucking brave

And Stephanie's smile makes you just believe
In yourself and in god and what's up your sleeve
Samantha is generous with pure heart so kind
She'll lift you so high it will blow your mind

And Debbie I've known for 'bout twenty years
My god she shines, grown, defeating her fears

And Nadja she teaches me everyday
to create, be a mom, wife and friend come what may

Nicole makes me laugh with her ease of life
How she takes things in stride and finds something light

Vani my heart and my soul we are twins
Creative and glowing an always best friend

Erin, she's grounded and lends an ear
Her feedback is perfect so I can hear
Esmé my sweet little cutie pie
reminds me that childhood is where we fly

Amy my guide and my truth teller
This year I'd have sunk were it not for her
Emily's not just yoga she's like family yes
How we knew it was lifelong when we first met

Ekta a queen and pragmatic ideals
Her honesty, friendship and wisdom is real
Mirissa brings levity, humor and fun
No matter the place she's a loyal one

Marcy my neighbor my dancer in time
When i need a partner she's up for the crime

Maddie, the newest yet i've known her so long
She feels like a brother, a sister, a song

Adele is my sun and my moon and stars
When she sings the world stops from here to Mars

And me, who am I
without all the above?
I am nothing without all of my lady love.

I know – To Sam + Debbie
(a poem on life, death + new beginnings)

I know you are tired
I know your heart aches
I know you are restless
I know your life waits

I know babies crying
I know that it's late
I know you are weary
I know this is fate

I know you'll get through this
I know you'll be fine
I know sleepless nights come
I know sun will shine

I know every moment
I know we all learn
I know that you miss her
I know your eyes burn

I know that she visits
I know that she smiles
I know that she sees you
I know she's here while...

I know she is so proud

I know she loves you
I know sun is all her
I know moon is too
I know why I left him

I know that he's gone
I know he left long ago
I know we are done

I know my grief's chosen
I know it still hurts
I know we three heal most
I know we've found worth

I know we are warriors
I know we're divine
I know we'll pull through this
I know sun will shine.

  ♡ love

the end part...

My home is my friend

My house smells like pop-
corn
And riddles and rhymes
I feel kinda lonely
I'm just passing time

But be in the moment and
Try as I may
I just keep on reaching
For another day

Then that day will come
And pass with the wind
I'll start something fresh
And do it all again

Next day may be cookies
And candles and dreams
And next day a snuggle
A cuddle a scream

If god is my boyfriend
My best friend is me
Then why do i long for
Someone's company?

To doddle and squirm
And bump in the night
Companion and lover
It all feels so right

Then shame comes a crawlin'
Like critter to sea
I smoke and i clean
I ignore little me

But she needs my loving
My tender my heart
And she sleeps beside me
Protect her from dark

My house smells like cozy
Like healing love spells
I find myself smiling
Away go the bells

The quiet is comfort
The fountain is chime
And god is my boyfriend
My best friend is time

Time now not tomorrow
Time here in one place
I'm present i'm grounded
I take up the space

I breathe much more calmly
With paper to pen
My house smells like home
now
My home is my friend

Where you
ruin everything
came from
part...

the voice in my head

Me: Hello? This voice...do you have a name?

VOICE: I am you, you called me forward to get rid of this lie. I WANT TO SAVE YOU

Me: How are you saving me? Where are you even from?

Little Me: Truth... you ruin everything
You were the reason your parents got divorced. Your dad loved you more than your mom and your mom knew. She could not change it, she could not protect you.
You have been proving me right for years.

Me: Why would I, an adult woman, proudly self-sufficient ...care so much about what you say? Why are you so strong?....So mean?

LM: I am a survivor

Me: Yes...WE are, but I want to thrive...
Is there a way we can hold each other and not make it all so huge?

(just now heard a little kid and I'm annoyed, maybe that's why you're mean-i have been rolling my eyes at you for a long time)

LM: This new place is great, but lonely, so I'm scared, and I say mean things when I am scared.

Me: Same-I do too, maybe I can work on that too....show you you don't have to do that to "survive".

I TOOK ABOUT A 2 HOUR BREAK FROM WRITING TO HER AND WHEN I CRAWLED INTO BED HERE IS WHAT I HEARD AND FELT.

Me: I think you mean-I ruined everything. I gave up on your dreams! I hear you say it-and you are punishing me now, or think you can by saying that. It doesn't work sweet girl. But I know a better way-I do-we can find it together.

LM: I'll wait and see...

Me: It's about trusting myself! I won't let go of this authenticity-i am brave and ready to see YOU (her) and let everyone see US!

Wow-
Is there anything else?

LM: I feel safer now.
This is real, right?

Me: It is.
Yes
As real as it has ever been.

    I've got you.